No doubt you've been bombarded with "expert" advice from your parents, professors, and countless advisors. It's time you got advice you can really use— from fellow students who've been where you're headed.

All **Students Helping Students™** guides are written and edited by top students and recent grads from colleges and universities across the U.S. You'll find no preachy or condescending advice here—just stuff to help you succeed in tackling your academic, social, and professional challenges.

To learn more about **Students Helping Students™**
guides, read samples and student-written articles, share
your own experiences with other students, suggest a topic
or ask questions, visit us at
www.studentshelpingstudents.com!

We're always looking for fresh minds and new ideas!

Check out these other **Students Helping Students™** titles at your local or college bookstore, and online at Amazon.com, BN.com, Borders.com, and other book retailers!

Each one is packed with practical and useful advice from people who really know what they're talking about— **fellow students who've been where you're headed!**

NAVIGATING YOUR FRESHMAN YEAR

As if getting accepted wasn't hard enough, dealing with the ups and downs of your first year at college is a unique challenge you'll be glad you only have to face once. Pick up this guide and learn from first-hand experiences of dozens of college students who've survived their freshman year and lived to help you get through it without losing your mind. *($8.95)*

LEAPING FROM PUBLIC HIGH TO A TOP U.

You worked your butt off for years to do well in school and be accepted by a top university. Congratulations. But if you think that the toughest part is behind you, think again. Get advice from fellow students who've done what you're about to do. Pick up this guide to help you prepare for and tackle the academic, social, and personal challenges that you'll face as you make the transition from high school to a top university. *($6.95)*

GETTING THROUGH COLLEGE WITHOUT GOING BROKE

Figuring out how to pay for college and get through it without thousands of dollars of unnecessary debt is one of the toughest things you'll ever do. As the costs of education keep rising, you have to be more resourceful, creative, and persistent in finding money to pay for it, as well as learning how to manage the money that you've got. This guide is packed with specific advice from fellow students who've faced this challenge, made some mistakes, and can share their most valuable lessons with you. *($8.95)*

TACKLING YOUR FIRST
COLLEGE PAPER

Whether you wrote dozens of papers in high school or escaped without writing more than a few, acing your first few college papers will be a new and challenging experience. This guide will help you get ready, get organized, choose an interesting topic and a strong thesis, write a clear and error-free paper, and keep your sanity while you do it. *($6.95)*

SCORING A
GREAT INTERNSHIP

Finding and getting a killer internship during college has no downside— you'll learn a ton, spice up your resume, meet new people, and hopefully get a few steps closer to knowing what you'd like to do with your life after college. This guide is packed with tips on how to find the best internships, get yourself noticed and accepted, and how to learn the most once you're there. *($6.95)*

CHOOSE THE RIGHT COLLEGE &
GET ACCEPTED!

Figuring out where to go to college, writing essays, surviving interviews, doing well on tests, getting strong recommendations, figuring out how to pay for the ever-growing education price tag, dealing with parents, counselors, and countless advisors...all of that adds up to a good amount of stress, anxiety, and, most of all, hard work. This book is filled with practical advice and the personal experiences of dozens of students and recent grads who've succeeded in the college admissions process and share with you what they've learned. Pick up a copy for yourself and your best friend and ace your college applications without tearing out all of your hair. *($12.95)*

FIND YOUR PASSION
IN COLLEGE

Part of what college is all about is helping us to figure out what we like to do and what we might like to do with our lives. To really do this, you have to go beyond classes and academics, and explore your passions by getting involved in extracurriculars. Think you might like to be a journalist but hate your English class? Become a reporter for your college or local town paper. A life as psychologist sounds life fun? You won't learn much about it in your psych class, but might if you staff a counseling hotline. Pick up this guide and use it to help you find your passion. *($8.95)*

Students Helping Students™

TACKLING YOUR HIGH SCHOOL TERM PAPER

First Edition

NATAVI GUIDES

New York

120901

Tackling Your High School Term Paper.
First Edition.

Published by **NATAVI GUIDES**. For information on bulk purchases or custom promotional guides, please contact the publisher via email at sales@nataviguides.com or by phone at 1.866.425.4218. You can learn more about our promotional guides program on our website, www.nataviguides.com.

Cover design by Monica Baziuk.

Printed in the U.S.A.

ISBN 0-9719392-1-7

Library of Congress Cataloging-in-Publication Data

Tackling your high school term paper.-- 1st ed.
    p. cm. -- (Students helping students)
Primary author: Christina Zaroulis.
  ISBN 0-9719392-1-7 (pbk.)
  1. Report writing--Handbooks, manuals, etc. 2. Education, Secondary--United States. I. Zaroulis, Christina. II. Natavi Guides (Firm) III. Series.
  LB1047.3.T33 2002
  808'.02--dc21
                      2003010041

A NOTE FROM THE FOUNDERS OF
STUDENTS HELPING STUDENTS™:

Dear Reader,

Welcome to Students Helping Students™!

Before you dive head-first into reading this book, we wanted to take a moment to share with you where Students Helping Students™ came from and where we're headed.

It was only a few years ago that we graduated from college, having made enough mistakes to fill a *War and Peace*-sized novel, learned more and different things than we expected going in, and made some tough decisions—often without having enough advice to help us out. As we thought about our college experiences, we realized that some of the best and most practical advice we ever got came from our classmates and recent grads. It didn't take long for the light bulb to go off: We started a publishing company and launched the Students Helping Students™ series.

Our vision for Students Helping Students™ is simple: Allow high school and college students to learn from fellow students who can share brutally honest and practical advice based on their own experiences. We've designed our books to be brief and to the point—we've been there and know that students don't have a minute to waste. They are extremely practical, easy to read, and cheap, so they don't empty your wallet.

As with all firsts, we're bound to do some things wrong, and if you have reactions or ideas to share with us, we can't wait to hear them. Visit **www.StudentsHelpingStudents.com** to submit your comments online and find our contact information.

Thanks for giving us a shot. We hope that the student advice in this book will make your life better and easier.

Nataly and Avi
Founders of NATAVI GUIDES and Students Helping Students™

the primary author

Christina Zaroulis is the recipient of the Pfizer, Inc.
National Merit Scholarship. She tackled two term papers in
her high school career and graduated from the Groton
School magna cum laude in June, 2001, having won
awards in both creative writing and the combined fields of
history and literature. She's a member of the Harvard
University class of 2006 and lives in New York City with her
parents, three siblings, two pups, and an old cat.

the contributors

Students and recent grads from the Brooks School,
Housatonic Valley Regional High School, Bowdoin College,
Colgate University, Columbia University, Cornell University,
Georgetown University, Harvard University, Middlebury
College, Princeton University, Stanford University,
Wesleyan University, and the University of Chicago
contributed their brutally honest advice, ideas, and
suggestions to this book.

author's note

When I first approached the writing of this book, I worried that the high school term paper was too broad a category to construct a blueprint for writing a variety of papers that we might encounter in high school. Term papers are assigned in many subjects, though most often in English and history, and a literature essay doesn't really resemble a paper written for a science class.

I soon realized, however, that I could create a blueprint for writing *any form* of high school term paper as long I could trust you, the reader, to remember to adapt and customize the advice you're about to read to your own needs. I intended this guidebook to be an outline for all those approaching the daunting and sometimes intimidating task of writing a term paper. I hope to help you avoid breakdowns or standstills, both of which I suffered when writing my own high school papers.

What this guidebook is by no means intended to do is stifle you or give you the idea that there is just one way to tackle your paper. There isn't, and as you read through the pieces of advice that follow, don't be afraid to alter the order of steps or the details to make this guidebook useful to you.

Good luck, and remember, you're in the driver's seat.

- Christina

contents

1

what it is

Your high school term paper is quite literally the paper you create over the course of an entire term, either a semester or a trimester. While it's usually a requirement for an English or history course, teachers of other high school subjects can and do assign term papers. Most high school students confront the term paper in their junior or senior year, or in an honors or Advanced Placement course, but even some freshmen have been known to tackle this surmountable giant.

The high school term paper's chameleon-like character cannot be denied: At times it makes us frustrated, at others proud. It drains us but gives us energy. It is both a huge bore and an interesting task, annoying and refreshing at the same time.

Whether it feels hot or cold, its important to always remember its true spirit: The high school term paper requires good quality and long-term work, in the form of research and the development of a thesis, and it culminates in the creation of a clearly written document. Its completion is rewarding and it assures us that we have developed some important planning and writing skills that will help us beyond high school, into college, and later in life.

The high school term paper requires, above all things, organization. It's impossible to stress enough the importance of getting and staying organized as you work on it. If you avoid the urge to jump in and just see where your efforts take you, you'll be half way to your goal of writing a killer term paper.

② what it's not

On one hand, the high school term paper is *not* that other high school paper that we threw off until the night before it was due, miraculously wrote without an outline in the hour before *Letterman* was on, and printed out on that hideous fluorescent orange paper, which just happened to be in the printer at the time. It is *certainly not* that short book report that we wrote in junior high. And it's *absolutely positively not* a paper that lacks all originality and presents loud and clear ideas and arguments that many others have argued over and over.

On the other hand, the high school term paper is not a dissertation or a graduate school thesis. It's not dozens of pages long (at least most of the time), it need not be based on thousands of pages of research, and it doesn't have to argue a completely original idea. Your term paper also doesn't have to be everything you do from the time it's assigned to the time you complete it. In fact, while you work on your term paper, you'll be assigned work in all of your other classes, including the one for which you're writing the term paper. Your term paper doesn't define your academic worth, and it certainly doesn't overshadow all of your other glorious high school feats.

Most importantly, it is *not* the enemy.

③

getting started

Whether you're anxious to start researching a topic you have in mind or are completely intimidated by the prospect of writing a term paper, your task will be much more manageable if you're organized before you start.

Get yourself together and lay out your strategy for how you can create the best possible term paper (to be handed in on time). Even for those of you who find organization a pain, or have gotten by with procrastination in the past, we promise that a good level of organization will make your life much easier as you confront this particular task.

MAKE A TIMELINE RIGHT AWAY
▼
COLLECT NECESSARY SUPPLIES
▼
GET TO KNOW YOUR RESEARCH FACILITIES

MAKE A TIMELINE RIGHT AWAY

As soon as your teacher assigns a term paper, you should step back, take a breath, shoo away any anti-term paper feelings, and schedule your time. This means you must deal with your assignment *early*.

You can compose a timeline by hand, as a Word document, or keep track of your term-paper-related tasks on your calendar or in your daily organizer. Your initial timeline should be forgiving and loose. Create time constraints for the six major steps of writing a high school term paper: choosing a topic, creating your thesis, researching, writing, revising, and finalizing your work.

Take your teacher's expectations into account. Length requirements will affect the time you allot for the composition of the paper. And always consider any sub-deadlines. For example, your teacher might require such things as handing in your thesis statement, a certain number of index cards, or your first draft of the paper for review. Make sure your timeline revolves around these concrete deadlines.

Your number one concern is obviously the due date for the paper, which is the end of your timeline. After all of your hard work the last thing you want is to be late in turning in your paper. You want your grade to reflect your work, not something as avoidable as an inability to manage your time. If certain circumstances require you to push back your paper's due date, make sure to talk to your teacher as early as possible.

COLLECT NECESSARY SUPPLIES

Collect whatever supplies you'll need to work on your paper before you begin. If you have them around, you'll be more likely to use them and they'll make your work easier and more organized.

Buy index cards. Lots of index cards. Many of us are index-card shy, but to write a great term paper and stay sane as you do it, you'll need index cards. They are a great tool for keeping track of your research and organizing your points and arguments into an outline for your paper.

While you're roaming through your local office supply store you should also pick up an index card case—to match the size of your index cards, of course—and index card separators. You might even want to buy index cards in different colors and assign each color to a particular source or a particular part of your paper. Remember: Index cards are helpful, but well-organized index cards are even more helpful.

Also consider buying a large, three-ring binder to help you keep track of loose sheets of information, such as photocopies of articles for your research or handouts you get in class.

Author's corner
▾

Besides index cards, the only supply I believe is 100% necessary is a 3½ inch floppy disk or a CD, if your computer has a CD-ROM. You'll need to get into the habit of saving a back-up copy of your term paper somewhere other than your computer's hard drive every time you compose a new paragraph or complete a session of writing. A floppy disk or a CD work great as your back-up storage.
▴

GET TO KNOW YOUR RESEARCH FACILITIES

Whether you've spent endless hours in your high school library or have never set foot in it, now is the time to get re-acquainted or meet for the first time. Your librarian will probably be delighted to direct you to and explain your library's research tools: the card catalogue, computer system, archives, and other resources. Make sure you know how to use all of the available tools—you don't want to be wasting valuable time trying to get the microfiche machine to work.

Many teachers may actually take their students on a field trip to the library after assigning a term paper. Even if you think that you know all there is to know about using the tools in the library, take advantage of this refresher course and pay attention. You'll definitely appreciate it later on.

If your library lacks abundant research tools or has limited book stacks, you might want to consider finding an alternate research facility in your area, such as a local public library or a library at a nearby college or university. You should also ask your librarian whether your library can borrow books from other libraries, just in case you need a particular resource later on.

If possible, try to have access to the Internet to do some of your research. If you can harness your willpower and limit the diversions that the Internet has to offer, it will serve as an extremely valuable research tool. Perhaps the most useful websites you'll find are those that allow you to access the text from thousands of books and magazine and newspaper articles online, such as **www.Questia.com**.

"Students should not be afraid to ask for assistance from their teachers outside of class time. Get a jump on everyone else and begin your paper right away. The early bird will get the worm (teacher's help) before the masses come begging for help at the eleventh hour."

**Honors English Teacher,
Foothill High School**

4

choosing
a topic

Since you'll be spending a great deal of time working on your term paper, it's a good idea to take some time to carefully think about your topic. You'll want to choose one that is intriguing to you in some way and can sustain your interest for several months. You'll also want to choose a topic that's manageable enough to research thoroughly in the time allotted and using the research tools you have at your disposal.

Below are a few suggestions for what you might want to consider as you think about your topic.

DISTINGUISH BETWEEN TOPIC AND THESIS
▼
SHOP AROUND
▼
CHOOSE A TOPIC YOU ENJOY
▼
FIND ENOUGH RESEARCH FOR YOUR TOPIC

DISTINGUISH BETWEEN TOPIC AND THESIS

Before you dive into thinking about your topic, make sure that you know the difference between a topic and a thesis. A topic is the general subject of your paper, like a historical period, an economic concept, or a piece of literature about which you might write. To give you an idea, here are a few examples of what a topic might be:

- For an English paper, a topic might sound something like "Feminism Reflected in 20th Century American Literature."

- For a history paper, "Queen Elizabeth and the Church of England."

- For a sociology paper, "The Development of the African-American Ghetto."

The thesis of your paper is a position you will argue about your topic and one that you will support with evidence from your research. The thesis of the English paper we used as an example above might be something like:

- "Hemingway was one of the most feminist writers of all 20th century American authors."

(We don't actually recommend that you choose this as your thesis, however.)

When thinking about your topic, make sure that you choose a subject that's not too narrow and one about which you'll be able to argue a valid and interesting thesis position. (More on creating a strong thesis in the next chapter.)

SHOP AROUND

As soon as you hear that you'll be writing a term paper, a topic will probably pop into your head. Perhaps you've already read a few Jane Austen novels, were enamored by her strong female characters, and want to write your English paper on Jane Austen women. Or perhaps you want to know more about the fall of the Aztec Empire, the topic that was touched on—but not explored in depth—in your history textbook.

Even if you have a feeling about what you might want your topic to be, shop around for a bit before setting it in stone. You might find that the topic you'll enjoy researching the most was not the topic about which you first thought. To get ideas for a topic, flip through the material you've covered in the course for which your term paper was assigned. Also, check out the many reference books that suggest paper topics—you can usually find these in your library or local bookstore.

Approach your teacher with a few options that you like and get his or her opinion. Talk to your teacher about topics that other students have chosen in the past. Remember that a topic is broad and general, and writing on the same topic as another student is quite common. What you have to try and make original is your thesis, and you'll have plenty of opportunity to do this once you decide on the general topic of your paper.

In the end, you might choose the topic that your instincts suggested in the first place, but you'll feel confident you made the choice carefully.

CHOOSE A TOPIC YOU ENJOY

This piece of advice is probably obvious to you, but it's worth mentioning. For a few months you'll spend a significant amount of time slaving over your term paper. You might as well choose a topic that interests you and one about which you'll enjoy reading quite a bit of information.

Even though you might not think so now, having the opportunity to research and learn about an interesting topic can be fun and enjoyable. It's a nice break from regular class work and boring assignments, and you might even learn a thing or two in the process.

Another important reason to choose a term paper topic that interests you is that it will help you write a better paper and get a higher grade. Ever notice how you can remember every intricate bit of detail about your favorite TV show but can't recall the main point of a dull biology video? There's a reason for it: When you're interested in something you're more engaged by it. And if you're interested in your paper topic, you're more likely to be engaged and fully immersed in your research and arguments, which will make the final product quite stellar.

On the flip side, if you get bored by your topic you'll have a much harder time researching and thinking about it, and this will make it difficult for you to write an engaging and well-argued term paper.

> *"If you have the ability to pick your own topic, don't pick one that is necessarily the easiest but rather one that is most enjoyable. You will find your paper easier to write."*
>
> **Freshman,**
> **Colgate University**

You might find yourself in a situation where your term paper topic is pre-assigned. While you have less room to get creative and select a topic that interests you, you're not completely fenced in. A topic is something so broad and general that you'll definitely be able to find a few sides of it that are more interesting to you than others. And you'll always be able to formulate your own thesis about the topic, giving you the opportunity to make sure that your paper fits your interests at least in some way.

FIND ENOUGH RESEARCH FOR YOUR TOPIC

Once you've narrowed down your topic to two or three possibilities, don't finalize your choice until you're confident that there are enough resources at your disposal for researching it. Take some time to figure this out at the beginning, rather than getting stuck half way to your paper's deadline wishing you could start from scratch and choose a new topic.

Remember that one of the main things that your term paper is meant to test is your ability to conduct thorough research. You've got to make sure that your grade reflects your ability to do significant research and you're not left with too little information.

You've probably run across a few useful resources for your topic as you thought about what it might be. When you have a clearer idea, go back through your library's resources to see just how much information is available. Use the computerized card catalogue to search for sources using keywords related to your topic. Remember that if your school's library collection is limited, you might need to extend your search to a nearby public or university library.

After you have a list of sources, it might be a good idea to actually find a few of them on the shelves and look through their tables of contents and indices. Doing this will give you a good idea of how useful each source will be to your research.

Don't forget to look for relevant websites, documentaries, and magazine and newspaper articles on your topic. You'll need to make sure that your research is diverse and does not rely too much on any single source. We'll talk about this point in more detail later on, but as you look for sources on your topic, make sure that you can find a good variety of information from different types of sources.

"My advice? Number one: Find something you're interested in and read around the subject. Number two: Don't cheat and don't plagiarize."

**Head of the History Department,
Spence School**

5

formulating
a thesis

Before you dive into researching your paper topic, you have to complete one more very important step: figuring out what your thesis will be. A thesis is a position or claim about your topic that you'll argue in your paper and support with evidence from your research.

While it might be tempting to think that you'll figure out your thesis once you do your research, this is not the best approach. You already know some preliminary information about your topic—from class and from the work you did searching for your topic and research sources. Based on that information, you should try to formulate an argument about the topic. No doubt this position will change as you research and find supporting or opposing arguments, but having a preliminary thesis will help you focus your research, save time, and write a stronger and clearer term paper.

Here are a few suggestions for how to think about the thesis for your paper.

SKIM YOUR SOURCES
▼
ASK QUESTIONS ABOUT YOUR TOPIC
▼
AIM FOR AN INTERESTING AND VALID THESIS
▼
DISCUSS YOUR THESIS WITH OTHERS

SKIM YOUR SOURCES

"It's vital that you have a good thesis early on. If you don't, it just makes all the other steps nearly impossible."

Senior,
Housatonic Valley Regional High School

Think of this as the brainstorming portion of your research. Collect as many of your research sources as possible, grab a notepad, and skim through each source to figure out what your preliminary thesis might be. You've probably skimmed more than a few books in your high school career and have a method that works for you. One way you might try is to find the book's relevant sections in the table of contents and then read the introduction and first and last sentence of each paragraph.

As you skim, jot down the main ideas that you find about your topic. Also take note of any particular details that interest you or points that you think you might like to argue in your term paper. Don't lose track of why you're skimming. Your main goal is to formulate a position on your topic and make sure that it's a position you could reasonably argue using the research available to you.

"After finally completing my term paper, I realized that I'd become much better at skimming books and articles for information important to my topic instead of reading through entire books and not having any clue as to what I should do with all that material."

Freshman,
Bowdoin College

ASK QUESTIONS ABOUT YOUR TOPIC

One of the ways to develop a thesis is to ask questions about your topic. Going through this exercise as you skim through your sources will help you nail down a good thesis.

Here's an example. Suppose John is writing a term paper on the topic of Bill Clinton during his Monica Lewinsky scandal years. John does a bit of research on the topic, learns about the blue dress, the oval office engagements, and figures he wants to write something about Bill Clinton's perspective on the situation. He formulates a question he finds intriguing, something like: "Did Bill Clinton understand the consequences of his actions?"

After thinking about what he's read in his research so far, John formulates a position as an answer to the question: "Yes, Bill Clinton did comprehend what he was doing, but he didn't fully appreciate the gravity and the implications of his actions."

John's answer to the question can now become a thesis for his term paper on Bill Clinton and his perspective on his relationship with Monica Lewinsky. While we don't recommend that you ever write a paper on this worn-out topic, we included this example to help illustrate how posing a question about a topic can lead to a thesis for your term paper.

AIM FOR AN INTERESTING AND VALID THESIS

"Although you don't have to be completely original in your paper and develop some intricate thesis that no one before has ever conceived, you do need to

make sure that your paper has an interesting argument, not just a summary of events. "

**Freshman,
Princeton University**

Just because you can ask and answer a question about your topic doesn't mean that you've come up with a strong and valid thesis. Notice how in talking about what a thesis is we've stayed away from calling it an opinion. That's because a good and valid thesis is more than just your personal opinion on a certain topic. A good thesis is an opinion that can be argued and supported using evidence and information from a variety of sources.

Not all positions or opinions can be successfully argued and supported with evidence. Some ideas are so well accepted that there aren't many arguments that oppose them. And if no one could argue against your thesis then it doesn't make for a great issue about which to write your paper. On the flip side, you also don't want to choose a thesis for which you can't find any supporting evidence.

Teachers are rarely impressed with shocking or extremely unique theses that we can't support well in our papers. A better idea is to argue a thesis that is a somewhat original position on your topic and one for which you can find lots of supporting evidence and some opposing arguments from a variety of sources.

Let's say you're writing a term paper on "The Development of the African-American Ghetto," a hypothetical topic we mentioned earlier. Here are a couple of examples of not-so-great theses for this topic:

- "The formation of the African-American ghetto was a terrible event that would cause many of the urban poor future strife."

This thesis is extremely broad and general and you'd be hard-pressed to argue it well in a term paper.

Here's another example:

- "A few hot Southern summers and the African-Americans' general discontent with farming caused the rapid formation of the African-American ghetto."

This thesis is not valid and cannot be supported strongly through research evidence.

Here's a thesis that might be a better choice for this paper topic:

- "The African-American Ghetto solidified in the 1940s and 50s as a direct result of the invention of the mechanical cotton picker in 1944 and the 'Black Migration' from the Southern plantations that followed."

This thesis is debatable, interesting, and you can find ample evidence to argue and support your position.

DISCUSS YOUR THESIS WITH OTHERS

Don't be shy to talk about your thesis with your teacher and classmates. It's always a good idea to get someone else's thoughts both on your paper topic and your thesis because other people might think of issues and points that you haven't considered.

Try not to think about seeking outside opinions as a weakness. It's actually quite the opposite and it shows that you care about your paper and its quality. Your teacher will be pleased to see that you're treating the assignment thoroughly and with a high level of commitment, and you might find out a few things that will make your work easier.

As you talk to others about your thesis, tell them about the arguments you think you might use to support it. If they disagree or don't seem convinced by your reasoning, don't get defensive. Instead, go back to your notes and figure out whether you need to shift your position or one of its arguments, or whether you're still pretty confident that you can successfully support your thesis.

Get some advice, check with your teacher, but remember that this is your paper and your work. If you're passionate about a certain topic or thesis, don't give up easily even if others disagree.

Author's corner
▼

One of my papers became extremely painful to write when I realized that I was trying to prove a thesis that could not be proven. It became clear to me and I realized that if I'd asked just a few people about the validity of my thesis before I began, I would've saved myself much frustration and re-writing.

▲

"As you accumulate sources and begin taking notes, consider narrowing the topic. After gaining an overview of the topic, formulate a topic question—a specific question that you intend to answer. Also, presentation is key—no amount of sterling research will save a poorly presented paper."

History Teacher,
Groton School

6

researching your paper

The key to succeeding with your research and even enjoying it a bit is to have a plan before you begin. If you plan out how and which sources you will approach, have a system to help you keep track of your notes, and remember that you're researching for evidence and arguments related to your paper's thesis, you'll avoid pitfalls like running out of time or drawing too much information from a limited amount of sources.

Check out our suggestions for conducting your research below and remember to try and have some fun with it.

RESEARCH WITH A PURPOSE

▼

USE INDEX CARDS

▼

MIX IT UP

▼

REFER BACK TO YOUR THESIS

▼

ENJOY YOUR RESEARCH

▼

TIME YOURSELF

RESEARCH WITH A PURPOSE

While it's important to enjoy your research, you have to keep in mind that you're flipping through dozens—or hundreds—of pages for a reason. You're doing it to understand the relevant issues and details as they relate to your topic, and more specifically, you're searching for evidence to support the thesis of your term paper. Since there are many other things you'd like to do besides sitting in the library, keep your focus so you can get out of there sooner.

Because you've already skimmed through many of your sources, you should have no problem getting the most relevant information from a source and moving on. It might be a good idea to develop a systematic way to approach each source.

Here's one way to do this with a book, but you should feel free to create your own:

- Check the book's table of contents to find the most relevant sections.

- Skim through the introduction. This is usually the roadmap to the book and it will help you focus on its key sections.

- After you find the relevant chapters or sections, read them and take notes. Write down enough information so it will make sense to you when you read it later, but avoid copying sentences word for word. (And make sure that you always indicate from which source the information is coming.)

- Check out the bibliography—if there is one—to see what other related sources you might want to read.

Don't waste too much time reading through the parts of your sources that aren't helpful in developing good arguments for your term paper. No one is going to count how many pages you read or care whether you read each of your sources from start to finish. What matters most is that you maximize the use of your time and learn the relevant information about your topic.

USE INDEX CARDS

Whether you're a whole-hearted, anti-index-card-activist or someone who has used index cards regularly, your best bet is to use them as you research your paper. Don't feel like your teacher's requirement to use index cards is meant to constrict your free spirit or dictate how you should learn. It's a good suggestion and one that's echoed by most students, some of whom wish they'd used index cards as they look back on a few bad term paper experiences.

"Note cards are key. I wrote two big term papers in my high school career: one of them I wrote without cards, the other with. For the one without note cards, I ended up getting confused about my notes and where I actually found my information. Writing down my research on paper didn't give me the crucial ability to organize my thoughts before I began to write. On the other paper, I ended up doing much better—proof that note cards can be really helpful!"

**Freshman,
Harvard University**

But don't just use index cards, use them well:

- Limit one idea, piece of information, or quotation to a single index card. If you fill up an entire card with text, it's likely that all of the information on that card will not be useful for the same section or paragraph of your term paper. When you finish your research and want to organize your index cards to format your paper, you'll find yourself wanting to cut full index cards in half. And who wants to spend time doing that?

- Assign a number to each source and make up a separate index card with bibliographic information about that source (more on that below). Include the source number on each index card to make sure that you always know from which source each piece of information is coming. Keeping track of the origin of each point will make it easy for you to go back and find additional information if you have to.

- You might also find it useful to make a short note to yourself about where in your paper the information on each card might be used. Since you've already thought about your thesis and some supporting arguments you'll want to use to argue it, you have a general idea of your paper in mind. When you use your index cards to create an outline for your paper later on, you'll save time by remembering where you thought each point would be most useful.

- Avoid writing down whole sentences word for word as you read them in your source. Not only does this put you at risk of plagiarism, but it takes too much time and isn't really necessary. When you do find relevant information, read through it, summarize the central point, and write that point down on an index card. If there is something more specific, such as a number, word, or any other type of evidence that you'll need to quote exactly in your paper, you'll want to write that down as well. (Make sure to indicate when something is an exact quote and when it's your own paraphrase because you'll have to differentiate between the two clearly in your paper.)

- Try to make your index cards look similar and be sure that they contain the same type of information. Each card should have: the source number, notes, page numbers, and reference to where in your paper that information might be most useful. If you create a single format for your cards you'll have a much easier time reading the information later on.

☞ A NOTE ON KEEPING TRACK OF YOUR RESEARCH

There's no way we can say this too much: Make sure that you keep track of all your sources. The last thing you want to be doing the night before your paper is due is searching through the library to figure out where you found that great point for your second paragraph. Keeping track of your research is easy if you create a simple system and stick to it.

One way to keep track of your sources is to create an index card with information about each source. Write down its title, author, publisher, date of publication, and which edition it is. You'll also find it useful to write down where this particular source is physically located—the library, your room, your locker, etc.

Invariably, there will come one day when you spend hours looking for that article you absolutely must re-read. Having a good system to keep track of all your research will help minimize the number of hours you spend looking for it.

MIX IT UP

As you research, make sure that you don't take a disproportionate amount of your material from one single source. Doing this will make you bored, make your paper limited in scope and biased, and make your teacher give you a lower grade. Force yourself to find, read, and draw from many different sources.

Relying too much on a single source might be difficult to resist at times, especially if you find that one great source that just seems to have all of the arguments and points laid out for your term paper. Don't succumb to the temptation. If you base your paper on a small number of sources, it will be extremely limited and may run the risk of sounding like a re-write of one of your sources. Remember, research is there to support your own arguments, not make them for you.

Mix up your resources. Make sure that you're getting information from a variety of books and articles and that you're not relying too much on information in any one of them. Also try to include a good balance between primary and secondary sources. You've probably learned about these already, but here's a refresher:

Primary Sources	Documents and records created and left behind by the participants of historical events, such as letters, diaries, manuscripts, and newspaper articles written at the time of these events.
Secondary Sources	Interpretations of primary sources created after certain events took place. A history textbook is an example of a secondary source.

REFER BACK TO YOUR THESIS

It's pretty easy to get caught up in your reading and note-taking and lose track of the core thesis of your paper. As you research, refer back to your thesis on a regular basis and make sure that you're always researching relevant points. If you don't, you run the risk of going off on tangents in your research that don't serve the purpose of providing evidence and support for your paper's main argument.

At some point, you might find that you need to alter or completely change your thesis. Perhaps you're not able to find enough supporting evidence for your thesis. Or maybe you find much more evidence opposing your thesis than supporting it. Of course, every thesis will have counter-arguments and you'll probably want to include a few of these in your paper. But if you can't find any information to support your main point and tons of information that refutes it, you'll need to reconsider your thesis.

Don't panic or get frustrated with yourself for choosing the thesis that you did and don't be afraid to change it part-way through your research. The point behind research is either to support the validity of your thesis or to find information that leads you to change it to a different position.

And this is why it's critical to always refer back to your thesis and keep track of what your research is showing about it. If you do this consistently, you'll likely avoid finding out a week before the paper deadline that you don't have enough evidence to support your thesis.

Try this: Write down your thesis statement on an index card and read it from time to time as you research. If you change your position, re-write your thesis.

ENJOY YOUR RESEARCH

There's no reason why your research can't be fun. In fact, many students to whom we spoke told us that research was a surprisingly interesting and enjoyable part of their work. Having an opportunity to spend dedicated time learning in depth about a topic of interest is truly a good thing and you should make the most of it.

Author's corner
▼

For one of my papers, I interviewed an elderly woman with whom I shared our apartment building for more than ten years. We'd never struck up a conversation before, and I got the chance to learn about her fascinating life. I really enjoyed it—as well as the Scottish shortbread cookies she served me— and it was one of the best things about doing my research.
▲

If you feel that your research is stressing you out or boring you, try to change the pace and setting in order to refresh your mind and get energized. Reading in a quiet library for hours a day can frustrate everyone. Find a different place to do your research and make sure that it's comfortable and conducive to focused reading. Spend some days reading in your own room, in a café, or outdoors, if you can concentrate.

There's no reason to feel confined to any one place or to feel like you have to do your research where everyone else is doing it. By seeking out or creating your own space for research, you'll be able to enjoy it more and get through it more efficiently.

Also, make sure that you take breaks from your reading. If you start your research early, you'll have plenty of time to take regular breathers and give your mind a research-free day at least once a week.

TIME YOURSELF

All good and bad things must come to an end, including your research. Whether you're enjoying it so much that you lose track of time, or you hate it so much that you put it off until the last moment, you might run into trouble. Make sure that you're always keeping track of your timeline and due dates.

If you find that you're running short on time but still have many sources left that you want to read through, consider skimming those sections that you otherwise might've liked to read more thoroughly. You'll have to get a bit more strategic in choosing what you read and what you skip, but you should be able to judge what matters most for your paper. And as you sprint through the last yards of your research, don't give in to the temptation to stop using index cards—you'll definitely thank yourself later on.

7

writing your term paper

While the actual writing of your term paper might be the most daunting part of the process, the hardest part is to begin writing. The blinking cursor at the top of a blank computer screen is no one's friend. Once you dive in and begin to write, however, you'll find that all the hard work you did researching and keeping track of information on index cards will make your task much easier.

Make sure to leave yourself more than a few days to write your paper and dive into it.

USE YOUR INDEX CARDS
▼
DON'T GET STUCK ON THE INTRO
▼
CREATE STRONG TOPIC SENTENCES
▼
STICK TO YOUR THESIS
▼
CAREFULLY ORGANIZE YOUR ARGUMENTS
▼
BE FAIR AND CONVINCING
▼
DON'T OVERUSE EVIDENCE
▼
GIVE CREDIT GENEROUSLY
▼
WRITE A "WOW" CONCLUSION
▼
END WITH A BIBLIOGRAPHY
▼
DON'T LET THE COMPUTER BRING YOU DOWN

USE YOUR INDEX CARDS

There was actually a good reason for creating all those index cards—they'll be a huge help as you begin to organize and write your term paper. Before you sit down at a computer, arrange your index cards in the order in which you'll use their information in your paper. One way to do this is to separate your note cards in piles. Each pile can stand for one paragraph of your paper or one section consisting of multiple paragraphs.

> *"I literally arranged my note cards in twenty thousand different orders, but once I had a good one, I copied their info down and there was my paper. Essentially, my note cards were my paper."*
>
> **Freshman,**
> **Georgetown University**

Once you've organized your index cards, you might want to create a brief outline of your paper. Some students and teachers believe that a detailed outline is an essential tool for writing a stellar paper. If you're one of those people, then go ahead and create a detailed outline using your index cards. But we think that a clear and brief outline of your main arguments is all you need to get going. An outline is there to guide you, not overwhelm you. Think of it as a snapshot of your paper. As you write, you can use your brief outline to make sure that you're staying on track.

At the end of this section we've included a simple template that you can use to structure your outline, but you should use whatever method works best for you.

One note of caution: Don't overburden your outline with too much detail. It can become overwhelming and you're better off spending your time actually putting the detail into your paper.

☞ SAMPLE OUTLINE TEMPLATE

Here's a simple template that you can use to begin to outline the main structure of your paper.

Thesis Statement

Argument One

1. Main point

2. Main supporting points
   a.
   b.
   c.

3. Key sources

4. Key data, quotes, statistics

Argument Two

1. Main argument

2. Main supporting points
   a.
   b.
   c.

3. Key sources

4. Key data, quotes, and statistics

Repeat for all arguments of your paper.

DON'T GET STUCK ON THE INTRO

You've probably heard this before: You don't need to begin your paper from the beginning. Think about it. The purpose of your introduction is to give the reader an overview of your thesis and main supporting arguments as you will present them in your paper. If you write the core of your paper first, your introduction can easily follow its flow and structure.

Some of us are order fanatics and absolutely, positively cannot proceed with the rest of the paper unless we write the introduction first. This is fine, too, just remember that you'll have to come back and refine it after you complete your paper. You shouldn't feel stifled by the introduction—it's actually the easiest part of your paper to write.

One good hint for a strong introduction to your term paper is to have its last few sentences be your thesis statement. You've probably seen the cone diagram in your writing class before: The introduction starts broad and general, goes through the main issues of the paper, and then culminates in a single point, the thesis. Depending on what type of paper you're writing, this may or may not work for you, but do consider it.

CREATE STRONG TOPIC SENTENCES

Your goal is to write a clear and well-argued paper that your reader can follow and understand as well as you do—but without having had the benefit of reading through pages and pages of research. You are your reader's guide through the arguments and points that support your thesis. You create the structure of your paper and have to show your reader the way through it. One great way to do this is to always write strong topic sentences for each of your paragraphs and sections.

A strong topic sentence prepares the reader for what's to come in the body of that particular paragraph. It also connects that paragraph to the overall thesis of the paper, indicating whether you're about to present a supporting argument, an opposing viewpoint, or a particular piece of evidence.

Here's an example of a strong topic sentence in an essay about September 11th:

> "September 11th caused more significant and lasting emotional distress in school children all around the U.S. than many psychologists initially predicted."

This topic sentence is specific, it states what the main purpose of the paragraph is—to present some arguments and evidence to support this assertion—and it's not filled with too much detail.

The same paragraph in the same essay could have a pretty poor topic sentence such as this:

> "September 11th upset American schoolchildren."

This topic sentence is very broad and doesn't suggest to the reader what type of arguments or evidence the author will present.

STICK TO YOUR THESIS

You're probably getting really sick of us repeating this, but trust us, it's worth it: Make sure that every paragraph you write contributes to the overall purpose of your paper, which is to present and argue your thesis. This doesn't mean, of course, that every paragraph must refer to the thesis literally. In fact, avoid doing this or your paper will sound redundant.

Instead, make sure that each paragraph and section serves the general purpose of arguing your thesis. Avoid including irrelevant information on your topic, which doesn't make your paper stronger. Ask yourself: "Why is this important in order to argue my thesis?"

CAREFULLY ORGANIZE YOUR ARGUMENTS

Give some thought to the order in which you present the arguments supporting your thesis statement. It makes a difference. Generally, we remember the things we read first and last better than those we read in the middle. So you might want to put your stronger arguments as the first and last in your term paper.

Depending on the type of paper you're writing, there are other considerations. For example, if you're comparing and contrasting two issues or people you could structure your paper in two ways. One would be to write about the first issue in full, including all of the points of comparison and contrast, and then write about the second issue or person. Another way would be to compare and contrast the two issues side by side, taking one characteristic and writing about how it's presented in each of the two. You're in control of how you structure your paper, but just remember that there are many ways to do it and if one doesn't seem to work, you can find another.

"You should construct your term paper to resemb[e] a mathematical proof: Present your argument, A, then support A with B, which leads to C. Maintain and emphasize C with D. While one might have thought E was true, in fact A in hand with B, C, and D demonstrate that it's not."

**Freshman,
University of Chicago**

Whatever you decide to do, it's a good idea to use the outline template we discussed in the previous section and lay out your arguments in the order you choose. See if the order makes sense to you and decide whether it makes your thesis stronger. It should.

BE FAIR AND CONVINCING

Remember that a strong argument isn't one that completely ignores its opposing viewpoints. In fact, if you fail to present rival arguments to your thesis and the rationale behind them, your paper might appear biased and not very persuasive.

Instead, your best bet is to confront the opposing viewpoints head-on and then argue rationally and with supporting evidence why your thesis is the more appropriate position on the topic. Showing respect to your opponent actually elevates the strength of your own arguments and allows you to persuade the reader of your paper using logic and relevant research information.

You don't have to bash the other side. Get to know its arguments, present them, and then show why they don't work.

DON'T OVERUSE EVIDENCE

Always make sure that your paper is a reflection of your own opinions and an assertion of your thesis. A paper filled with excessive quotes and ideas from outside sources loses its strength and you as its author lose your own voice. Remember that you did research to find supporting information and evidence for your own thesis and arguments, and this shouldn't change as you write. Quotes and statistics and other supporting information should strengthen your own arguments, not replace them.

Trust your own intelligence and your ability to express strong and clear arguments. Use supporting information only when you need it to back up your points. Don't bore the reader with too much information, and make sure to let your own voice come through.

GIVE CREDIT GENEROUSLY

When you do use a quotation or paraphrase from another source, you must indicate it as such with a parenthetical reference, a footnote, or an endnote. Which method of citation you use depends on what your teacher requires and your own personal preferences.

Make sure to find out if there are format requirements for citing your sources before you begin to write and you'll avoid having to waste time redoing your work. And don't be afraid to include too many footnotes or endnotes—you can always take them out later.

The single most important reason to give credit each time it's due is to avoid plagiarism. Plagiarism is stealing someone else's words and ideas and presenting them as your own. It's an awful thing and you should never do it. You're smart enough not to have to.

On the flip side, you don't want to be wrongly accused of plagiarism. You don't need to put in citations for general knowledge: uncontested dates, the authors of major works of literature, and basic historical facts don't need citations, for example. Anything else that's not your own work needs a citation. If you're not sure, cite the source anyway. It's better to have a few unnecessary footnotes than be accused of plagiarism.

☞ A NOTE ON INTERNET PAPER SERVICES

Yup, you can get a term paper from the Internet. Numerous paper depositories have sprung up in the last few years offering you A+ papers on any topic and for any class. All you have to do is fork over a few bucks and you're done with your paper assignment. Easy, right?

Not really. First of all, how do you know that the papers offered by these services are any good? You don't know and you have no way of finding out. Why would you trust someone else to write a better paper than you could if you have no idea about who the author is?

More importantly, however, if you bought a paper from one of these Internet services and turned it in as your own, you'd be plagiarizing big time.

Some students say that they check out Internet paper services to get ideas about how other people have approached similar topics. This doesn't sound so bad. But the temptation to plagiarize from the paper you're reading can be too great if you like what you see—it's right in front of you, you have two days to write your paper, you have another final in a day, and it would be so easy just to copy whole sections from someone else's paper.

Have some faith in yourself and leave Internet papers to someone else. You're smart enough to write your own.

WRITE A "WOW" CONCLUSION

Your chance to diverge from your thesis is in your conclusion. Here you have the opportunity to do something a little different, to provide both a solid finish to your paper and extend your original argument further, to explore some of its implications beyond the scope that you covered in your paper.

Your conclusion is the last thing your teacher will read. Take a chance and make your conclusion more that just a drab summary of your paper. You can summarize in the first few sentences, but then explore a few tangents and relate them back to your thesis.

END WITH A BIBLIOGRAPHY

Check with your teacher on the required format for your bibliography, but make sure that you carefully construct one for your paper.

Remember that your bibliography must include not only the sources you used in your parenthetical references, footnotes or endnotes, but also any source that lent relevant background information to your paper as a whole.

DON'T LET THE COMPUTER BRING YOU DOWN

Save. Save. Save. Save. And then save again.

At all costs, don't let the computer be the cause of any stress as you work on your paper. Save your work on a floppy disk or a CD each and every time you write a new section, revise a paragraph, or even change a few words. Make sure that you label your files and your disks carefully, indicating the date of when you saved the files.

Print out paper drafts often, but keep them away from colored beverages and pets.

Author's corner

If you haven't yet seen a schoolmate running through the hallway in tears, having just had his computer eat his major term project minutes before it was due, you will. After assisting a friend with his paper debacle, I saved my paper a few extra times from that day on.

"Above all, make sure you keep good track of your sources so you put together a good and thorough bibliography."

**Former ESL Teacher,
Lowell High School**

8

revising
your paper

After you go through the hard work of organizing, researching, and writing the first draft of your term paper, revising it should be a breeze. But if you take this step lightly, you risk jeopardizing your efforts and receiving a lower grade than you deserve. A spelling mistake might seem like a minor issue that shouldn't affect your teacher's evaluation of your paper, but a few spelling mistakes and a grammar problem here or there do damage the flow and overall impact of your paper.

Hang in there for this last sprint home, and use the few suggestions below to help you get through it.

MAKE THREE DRAFTS AT A MINIMUM
▼
BE AN INDEPENDENT CRITIC
▼
CREATE STRONG PARAGRAPH TRANSITIONS
▼
CHECK GRAMMAR AND SPELLING
▼
USE THE ACTIVE VOICE
▼
HAVE SOMEONE ELSE READ YOUR PAPER
▼
DON'T BE AFRAID TO RE-WRITE

MAKE THREE DRAFTS AT A MINIMUM

After your first rough draft, you should plan on printing out at least two more drafts before turning in the final document. Having three drafts will give you a chance to do your revisions and edits in sequence and avoid getting overwhelmed. Remember, you're revising the content of the paper as well as its writing, and your best approach is to do these in sequence.

Print out your first draft and focus on revising the content of your paper. Read your thesis statement, and as you read through the following paragraphs, make sure that they express the points you need to argue and they do it well. If you created a short outline at the beginning of this process, refer to it at this point in order to check that the structure of your paper makes sense and supports your thesis.

Once you're convinced that the content of your paper is what it should be, print out the second draft, and begin to edit the paper's writing. At this stage of revisions you're looking at your paper with a magnifying glass, focusing on details such as clear, well-structured sentences that don't contain superfluous words. One important thing to look out for is varying sentence structure—if all of your sentences sound alike, your paper will be rather boring. So make sure that you alternate shorter and longer sentences, and you don't begin too many of your sentences in the same way.

After editing your paper's writing, print out the third draft. If you have time, take a day or two and don't look at it. Then, come back to your paper and read through it one last time. This is your final chance to catch any mistakes, so don't rush.

BE AN INDEPENDENT CRITIC

As you revise your paper, try to read it with a somewhat independent eye. This is not easy, of course, because it is your paper and you wrote it. But if you can force yourself to read your arguments as a reader not familiar with your paper and its topic, you'll gain a great perspective. You'll be able to find lapses in logic, poor connections and transitions, as well as grammar and spelling mistakes.

If you take a few days between the time you finish writing and begin revising it will help you be more independent as you revise. If you're organized you should be able to find some time to get away from your paper and return with a more critical eye.

CREATE STRONG PARAGRAPH TRANSITIONS

Make sure that the many paragraphs in your paper are well connected to each other as well as to your thesis. Remember, you're leading your reader through your paper and its arguments, and good transitions between paragraphs help you to do this.

When you read your paper, make sure that the last sentence of one paragraph has some connection with the first sentence of the paragraph that follows. Unclear transitions can make your paper hard to follow and confuse your reader.

CHECK GRAMMAR AND SPELLING

As confident as you might be in your writing, check your grammar and spelling carefully as you revise. We all lapse sometimes, and who knows what funky spellings your fingers created on the computer keyboard late at night. If you have a grammar question, don't be too proud to consult a writer's manual or your old elementary school grammar book. Reference books are especially great to check for punctuation rules. Whatever you do, don't fully trust your computer grammar check because they often follow strange grammar rules.

Similarly, don't rely on your computer's spell-check too much. While it can catch most spelling errors, nothing can replace your own careful eyes.

Read your paper thoroughly and pay attention to the spellings of words that your spell-check will miss: there vs. their, whole vs. hole, right vs. write. You get the point.

USE THE ACTIVE VOICE

The passive voice sounds weak, and weak isn't something you want your paper to be. While you don't have to eliminate it entirely, most of your sentences should be active. Here's a quick reminder:

Passive: "The passive voice was discussed by the author."

Active: "The author discussed the passive voice."

HAVE SOMEONE ELSE READ YOUR PAPER

If you have time before you have to turn in your paper, try to get someone other than you to read it: your parents, your younger brother, your best friend, your favorite teacher. It's extremely valuable to get an independent opinion even if it's just on a few pages of your paper.

When you ask someone to read your paper, tell him or her that you're looking for a general impression and that you'd like to know of the areas that you need to clarify or strengthen. If you can find someone who's willing to go a step further and actually edit your work, grab the opportunity and don't forget to give lots of thanks.

You probably don't want to ask the teacher from the class for which the term paper was assigned, but if your teacher offers to give you comments mid-way through your work, it might be very helpful.

Author's corner
▼
I particularly benefited from having my friends read one of my drafts. Because they were likely to know little about what I was writing, they were quick to point out what puzzled them.
▲

DON'T BE AFRAID TO RE-WRITE

"I think revising is the hardest step in writing a term paper because you have to dispose of ideas that you once thought were good ones."

**Senior,
Brooks School**

If you find sentences or even paragraphs in your paper that don't make sense, don't just leave them there because you're tired and want to rid yourself of the paper. You might be tempted to do this, thinking that the sentence or paragraph must have made sense when you wrote it. But that's not a good reason and you'll regret your decision later, especially if your grade is less than stellar.

Take a deep breath and force yourself to revise. Think about any problem areas and figure out a way to fix them. You might need to go back to your index cards or reread a part of a source or two. But don't chicken or lazy out of changing or even totally scrapping parts of your paper if you think you can make it better. You'll definitely thank yourself later.

9

putting on the final touches

Congrats! You made it through an enormous amount of hard work and effort and you're moments away from being able to pronounce what might sound like the best words you've said in a long while: "I'm done!"

Hang on for just a few more steps to make sure that your hard work is presented in a way that enhances it. Here are a few last-minute things to consider.

CHOOSE A STRONG TITLE
▼
CONSIDER USING AN ABSTRACT
▼
COVER YOUR BASES
▼
MAKE IT LOOK SPECIAL
▼
GET IT IN ON TIME

CHOOSE A STRONG TITLE

Make your term paper look polished and professional by giving it an appropriate title. Stay away from catchy phrases or titles that are four lines long, but do try to infuse some creativity into your title. After reading your title, the teacher should know the general topic that your paper will cover and have a hint of your position on that topic.

Either separate your title from the rest of the text by a few lines or include a separate title page with the title in bold or italics—with no citation marks or underlines—your name, and the date.

On the other hand, don't drive yourself crazy over your title. The choice you make is hardly monumental and it's unlikely that a poor title can negatively affect your grade.

CONSIDER USING AN ABSTRACT

If you're really ambitious, consider using an abstract to introduce your paper. An abstract is a short summary of the paper that appears right after the title page. If your paper is particularly long, an abstract is a good way to give your teacher a quick summary and provide a map of what's to come.

Talk to your teacher about using an abstract and find out if there is a particular format you should use.

COVER YOUR BASES

- Make sure that you staple all of your pages together in the correct order.

- Double check that your footnotes appear on the same page with the information they're citing.

- Check that you've printed out the final draft of your paper—not an earlier one you've since edited.

- Title comes first, then paper, then bibliography.

- Run one last spell check for sanity's sake.

- If you need to hand in your index cards, organize them by source.

- Make sure you've used the same font throughout the entire paper.

MAKE IT LOOK SPECIAL

Little details count. Consider presenting your paper in a clear plastic cover (you can find one in any office supply store). Print it on a high-resolution printer, if possible. Use good, clean paper.

Your teacher's initial impression of your paper is important and can work in your favor. Pay attention to these last few details and maximize your grade.

GET IT IN ON TIME

This isn't complicated: Get your paper in on time. Don't be late. Don't forget it at home on the day when you have to turn it in. And if you do forget it at home, beg and plead with someone to bring it to you. If you can't finish on time, make sure to talk to your teacher a few days before, not on the day when you have to turn it in.

You've worked too hard to mess this up. Get your paper in on time and exhale!

10

the
daily grind

Working on your term paper can be a challenge and there will definitely be a few days here and there when it's just too much. Here are a few suggestions to help you get through the experience with your sanity intact.

▸ROLL WITH THE PUNCHES

Even with superb organization, consistent effort, and seemingly smooth progress, you might succumb to a few pitfalls as you work on your term paper. You might notice that you wrote half of your index cards in the wrong format, lost track of what information came from which source, or spent an hour revising a section of an old draft. Or maybe you get a less-than-stellar interim grade on your rough draft and can't figure out where you went wrong.

A few frustrating moments or mistakes are inevitable. Expect them, and when they happen, don't dwell on them. Take a break, clear your thoughts, and then come up with a clear plan of how you'll tackle each one. Set aside two hours to rewrite your index cards in the right format, go back through the parts of your sources you used the most to link them to the information in your paper, take the revisions you made on an older draft and transfer them to the most recent one. Take actions and look forward, rather than thinking about what you could and should have done.

►DON'T DO IT FOR THE GRADE

No matter how well you focus and research and write your paper, there's always a chance that you won't end up with a grade that you feel reflects the quality of your work. You know this and we know this and it's not always fair, but it's sometimes just the way it is. This doesn't mean that you shouldn't push as hard as you can to make sure that your work is at its best.

In fact, you should always aim to do your best work because, in the end, you'll feel good about it and be proud of what you've achieved regardless of what grade you get. If you don't feel like you did a great job, but your teacher gives you an "A," you'll have a little conscience worm swarming in your head, making you feel less than awesome. On the flip side, if you do your best but get a grade you think is too low, you'll survive knowing that you put in your best effort.

As Hallmark-card-like as this might sound, you know that it's true, so don't just do it for the grade.

▶DON'T GET STUCK

Be your own motivator. If you get tired or frustrated or just plain bored, figure out a way to not get stuck in that particular unproductive state. Change what you're doing, where you're doing it, or how you're doing it. Take a break. Talk to your teacher. Talk to your classmates. Anything— just don't get stuck and expect someone else to come and pull you out.

> *"I set up a rewards system to give myself motivation to continue working. I would set goals for the day, week, or whatever other period, and every time I achieved a goal, I'd reward myself. For example, if I had to write four pages in one night, I'd tell myself, if you write two pages before dinner, you can watch Dawson's Creek."*
>
> **Freshman,**
> **Stanford University**

▶TAKE LOTS OF BREAKS

You absolutely have to get away from your paper from time to time. Consider it part of your work plan and make breaks part of your timeline. Shut off your computer, put away your index cards, and fill your mind with something completely unrelated to your term paper. When you get back to work, you'll be refreshed and focused and you'll be able to do what you have to do much more efficiently.

Do something fun when you take a break—go running, watch your favorite movie, play basketball, read a book—anything, as long as you enjoy it and it has absolutely nothing to do with your paper.

Author's corner
▾

I'm particularly fond of the sitting-on-the-floor-with-the music-blasting-in-my-room-and-painting-my-toenails kind of study break. I also like to release my energy at the gym, taking a walk with a pal, or lounging about and watching one of my all-time favorite movies.

▴

11

helpful
resources

We've sifted through dozens of writers' guides and reference books to find a few that we think are most helpful in your quest towards a great term paper.

☞ BOOKS

10,000 Ideas for Term Papers, Projects, Reports, and Speeches: Intriguing, Original Research Topics for Every Student's Need, by Kathryn Lamm. ARCO Books, 1998.

Whether you're looking for ideas for a term paper on Twentieth Century History, Foreign Policy, or even Nutrition, this book suggests 10,000 solid paper topics.

MLA Handbook for Writers of Research Papers, by Joseph Gibaldi. The Modern Language Association of America, 5th Edition, 1999.

This book has been guiding students through all the technicalities of writing a research paper for over thirty years. It is particularly useful for learning how to properly format footnotes, endnotes, and the bibliography.

Writing with Sources: A Guide for Students, by Gordon Harvey. Hackett Publishing, 2000.

If the MLA Handbook appears daunting—it is—this short,

clear, and less expensive booklet is another resource that will help you to correctly document your sources.

Write Right: A Desktop Digest of Punctuation, Grammar, and Style, by Jan Venolia. Ten Speed Press, 2001.

Brushing up on your rules of grammar can be dull, but this book's wit and fun arrangement masks the bore of grammar. This booklet succinctly gives punctuation and mechanical advice. The "Confused and Abused Words" section demystifies the difference between capital and capitol, emigrate and immigrate, and answers many of the questions for which we can never find a clear answer.

☞ WEBSITES

www.questia.com

Questia is the largest online library and a fabulous resource. Simply run a search on your topic and you'll find a plethora of sources worth considering. It also aids the process of writing a term paper by helping you with everything from choosing a paper topic to formatting your bibliography.

www.bigchalk.com

bigchalk is "The Education Network," and their site has helpful resources for students of all ages. Check out the high school student area for some essay-writing tips, as well as a whole bunch of other topics, including proofreading and improving your study and research skills.

①②

the
final word

Sitting down to write this last section, I couldn't find inspiration for inspirational closing remarks. I tried out a few ideas, but they all amounted to nothing. Frustrated, I did as I often do when under pressure—I tied up my running shoes and went for a long jog in the beautiful park near my house.

As I ran, my inability to complete this last section reentered my mind no matter how hard I tried to separate myself from it. In my oxygen-deficient state, however, it suddenly became clear to me that a casual jog is a perfect —however cheesy—metaphor for writing a high school term paper:

Just stay loose on the flatways; accelerate on the downhills; keep it steady on the uphills.

Setting small goals for yourself will help the time pass and ensure the achievement of your goal.

Add some variety to your course with intervals—do some sprints between longer endurance pieces.

Make sure you take all the necessary precautions to avoid injury.

Finally, remember that no matter how badly it hurts when you're in the middle of it, your satisfaction and pride at the end will certainly outshine your past pain.

- *Christina*

To learn more about **Students Helping Students™** guides, read samples and student-written articles, share your own experiences with other students, suggest a topic or ask questions, visit us at **www.studentshelpingstudents.com**!

We're always looking for fresh minds and new ideas!